Covering the Bases:

Quotations on Baseball

Covering the Bases:

Quotations on Baseball

Edited by Paul E. Gangi

BARNES
&NOBLE
BOOKS
NEW YORK

Compilation copyright © 2003 by Barnes & Noble, Inc.

2003 Barnes & Noble Books

ISBN 0-7607-4056-9

Printed and bound in the United States of America

M 9 8 7 6 5 4 3 2 1

PLAYED WITH FERVOR FOR THE LAST TWO CENTURIES, the game of baseball has inspired a multitude of reactions—many of which you'll find gathered in this collection. Covering the Bases includes hundreds of quotes about our national pastime that are in turn insightful, moving, humorous, and sarcastic.

What comes through again and again from the quotes is that baseball is so much bigger than the game: It is a catalyst for conversation. It is played during prosperous times and economic depression, peace and war, day and night, good weather and bad, by the rich and poor, nationally and internationally. And it is a game that grips its fans like no other. We follow our teams through the long season and, for a lucky few, into the post-season. We witness the wins, the losses, the streaks, the slumps, and the blown games. We revel in their success and agonize in their defeats.

Perhaps the passion and fervor for the game is best expressed by A. Bartlett Giamatti who said that baseball, "is designed to break your heart. The game begins in spring, when everything else begins again, and blossoms in the summer, filling the afternoons and evenings, and then as soon as the chill rains come, it stops and leaves you to face the fall alone."

Anything else I could say would surely be a repetition of some of the memorable insights and reactions that have already been said about baseball. So read on and enjoy some perspectives on the game from some very wise and funny people.

–Paul E. Gangi
Brooklyn Heights, NY, 2003

The
Great Ones

Fans, for the past two weeks you have been reading about the bad break I got. Yet today I consider myself the luckiest man on the face of this earth. I have been in ballparks for seventeen years and have never received anything but kindness and encouragement from you fans... So I close in saying that I may have had a tough break, but I have an awful lot to live for.

—LOU GEHRIG, Hall of Fame first baseman, in his farewell speech at Yankee Stadium, July 4, 1939

Don't look back. Something might be gaining on you.

—SATCHEL PAIGE, Hall of Fame pitcher and Negro League great

"Mr. Rickey, do you want a ballplayer who's afraid to fight back?"

"I want a ballplayer with guts enough not to fight back!"

— Conversation between JACKIE ROBINSON and BRANCH RICKEY upon Robinson's signing with the Brooklyn Dodgers in 1947

Bob Gibson is the luckiest pitcher I ever saw. He always pitches when the other team doesn't score runs.

— TIM MCCARVER, all-star catcher, on his Cardinals' teammate

I'd like to thank the good Lord for making me a Yankee.

— JOE DIMAGGIO, Hall of Fame outfielder

One of the beautiful things about baseball is that every once in a while you come into a situation where you want to, and where you have to, reach down and prove something.

—NOLAN RYAN, Hall of Fame pitcher

When I began playing the game, baseball was about as gentlemanly as a kick in the crotch.

—TY COBB, Hall of Fame outfielder

I don't room with him; I room with his suitcase.

—BIG BODIE, on the late-night antics
of his roommate Babe Ruth

People ask me what I do in the winter when there's no baseball. I'll tell you what I do. I stare out the window and wait for spring.

—ROGERS HORNSBY, Hall of Fame second baseman

A team is where a boy can prove his courage on his own. A gang is where a coward goes to hide.

—MICKEY MANTLE, Hall of Fame outfielder

Baseball is a game, yes. It is also a business. But what it most truly is, is disguised combat. For all its gentility, its almost leisurely pace, baseball is violence under wraps.

—WILLIE MAYS, Hall of Fame outfielder

It's a great day for a ball game; let's play two!

—ERNIE BANKS, Hall of Fame shortstop
nicknamed "Mr. Cub"

Doctors tell me I have the body of a 30 year old. I know I have the brain of a 15 year old. If you've got both, you can play baseball.

—PETE ROSE, all-star outfielder

Anytime you think you have the game conquered, the game will turn around and punch you right in the nose.

—MIKE SCHMIDT, Hall of Fame third baseman

Hitting is timing. Pitching is upsetting timing.

—WARREN SPAHN, Hall of Fame pitcher

For years I have said my motivation for playing wasn't for fame and fortune, but rather the love of competing. Baseball is a team sport and I have been lucky enough to contribute to the success of some great teams.

—MARK McGWIRE, first baseman, from his retirement speech on November 12, 2001

There ain't much to being a ballplayer, if you're a ballplayer.

—HONUS WAGNER, Hall of Fame shortstop

I never realized that batting a little ball around could cause so much commotion.

—STAN MUSIAL, Hall of Fame outfielder/first baseman

I don't want them to forget Ruth, I just want them to remember me!

—HANK AARON, Hall of Fame outfielder
and home run champion

It ain't over 'til it's over.

—YOGI BERRA, Hall of Fame catcher

Cool Papa Bell was so fast he could get out of bed, turn out the lights across the room and be back in bed under the covers before the lights went out.

–JOSH GIBSON,
on Negro League speedster James Bell

A Taste of Champagne—
Views on Victory

Nice guys finish last.

— LEO DUROCHER, Hall of Fame manager

I never did say that you can't be a nice guy and win. I said that if I was playing third base and my mother rounded third with the winning run, I'd trip her up.

— LEO DUROCHER, Hall of Fame manager

Somebody's got to win and somebody's got to lose—and I believe in letting the other guy lose.

— PETE ROSE, all-star outfielder

Winning isn't the only thing. But wanting to is.

— JIM "CATFISH" HUNTER, Hall of Fame pitcher

When you're a winner you're always happy, but if you're happy as a loser you'll always be a loser.

—MARK FIDRYCH,
all-star pitcher nicknamed "The Bird"

I think winning is a learned behavior. I put a lot of weight behind the fact you have experience, because I really think it eliminates the unknown. You know what it's like.

—JOE TORRE, player and manager

I became an optimist when I discovered that I wasn't going to win any more games by being anything else.

—EARL WEAVER,
Hall of Fame manager for the Baltimore Orioles

I come to play. I come to beat you. I come to kill you.

—LEO DUROCHER, Hall of Fame manager

If I'd known I was gonna pitch a no-hitter today, I would have gotten a haircut.

—ROBERT "BO" BELINSKY, journeyman pitcher

When we lose, I can't sleep at night. When we win, I can't sleep at night. But when we win, I wake up feeling better.

—JOE TORRE, player and manager

When you win, you eat better, sleep better, and your beer tastes better. And your wife looks like Gina Lollobrigida.

—JOHNNY PESKY, all-star shortstop immortalized by Fenway Park's right-field foul pole, "Pesky's Pole"

If we lost, I'd be eating my heart out. But since we won, I'll only eat one ventricle.

—RON SWOBODA, outfielder from 1969 World Champion New York Mets

In modern baseball the winning equation is Power + Pitching = Pennant.

—BILL VEECK, baseball executive

Our goal going into the season is to win the World Series. Our goal isn't let's make the play-offs this year, or let's win the AL pennant. If we don't win the World Series, the season is a failure.

— DEREK JETER, Yankee shortstop and owner of several World Series rings

Yeah, I'm pretty good on 670 days of rest.

> —JOE MAGRANE, pitcher who was
> unable to post a win in two years

It only took me 21 runs and five years to get a win here.

> —ANDY PETTITE, pitcher commenting on
> his first win against the Texas Rangers
> in his home state of Texas

To the Showers—
Views on Defeat

Wait 'til next year.

—LAMENT OF THE BROOKLYN DODGER FAN

I have trouble remembering my wedding anniversary, but I remember those four pitches. I remember I got a big hand from the crowd when I left.

—PAUL FOYTACK, pitcher who gave up
four straight home runs in a single inning

Slumps are like a soft bed—they're easy to get into and hard to get out of.

—JOHNNY BENCH, Hall of Fame catcher

The only way to prove that you're a good sport is to lose.

—ERNIE BANKS, Hall of Fame shortstop

Come out and see my Amazin' Mets. I been in the game a hundred years but I see new ways to lose I never knew existed before.

—CASEY STENGEL, Hall of Fame manager
and manager of the 1962 Mets

When all is said and done, all I want anyone to say of me is, Earl Weaver—he sure was a good sore loser.

—EARL WEAVER, Hall of Fame manager
for the Baltimore Orioles

How can a guy win a game if you don't give him any runs?

—BO BELINSKY, pitcher, after losing a game 15-0

My baseball career spanned almost five decades from 1925–1973, count them, and in all that time I never had a boss call me upstairs so that he could congratulate me for losing like a gentleman. When you're playing for money, winning is the only thing that matters. Show me a good loser in professional sports, and I'll show you an idiot. Show me a sportsman, and I'll show you a player I'm looking to trade.

—LEO DUROCHER, Hall of Fame manager

If a tie is like kissing your sister, losing is like kissing your grandmother with her teeth out.

—GEORGE BRETT, Hall of Fame infielder and first player to win a batting title in three separate decades

Sometimes I think I'm in the greatest business in the world. Then you lose four straight and I want to change places with a farmer.

—JOE MCCARTHY, Hall of Fame manager who won seven World Championships with the Yankees

The last time the Cubs won the World Series was in 1908. The last time they were in one was 1945. Hey, any team can have a bad century.

—TOM TREBELLHORN, in 1994, after becoming the new manager of the Chicago Cubs.

The latest diet is better that the Pritikin Diet. You eat only when the Cubs win.

—GEORGE SHEARING, jazz pianist

If there is such a thing as a good loser, then the game is crooked.

—BILLY MARTIN, player and manager

We were as flat tonight as people used to think the earth was.

—DANNY OZARK, manager of the Philadelphia Phillies

You can learn a little from victory. You can learn everything from defeat.

—CHRISTY MATHEWSON, Hall of Fame pitcher

We are not going to lose because of the pressure. If we lose, it's because the other team just out-played us, and that's been our philosophy all year.

—LOU PINIELLA, player and manager

I get over bad games right away. Sometimes I've let it go even before I've left the mound. That quick. Why? Because it's over. What can you do about it? Nothing. The only thing you can do is fight if you're still in the game. After that you can do nothing.

—MARIANO RIVERA, relief pitcher

4th Inning

A View From the Mound

Home plate is seventeen inches wide, but I ignore the middle twelve inches, I pitch to the two-and-a-half inches on each side.

—WARREN SPAHN, Hall of Fame pitcher

Half the plate belongs to the batter, and half the plate belongs to me. That's fair. It's just that I never let the batter know which half is mine.

—DON DRYSDALE, Hall of Fame pitcher

My earned run average is so high it looks like an AM radio station.

—JIM GOTT, journeyman pitcher

It helps if the hitter thinks you're a little crazy.

—NOLAN RYAN, Hall of Fame pitcher

What they start, I finish.

— ROLLIE FINGERS, Hall of Fame relief pitcher

When Neil Armstrong first set foot on the moon, he and all the space scientists were puzzled by an unidentifiable white object. I knew immediately what it was. That was a home-run ball hit off me in 1937 by Jimmie Foxx.

— LEFTY GOMEZ, Hall of Fame pitcher

The bigger the game the better. I'm an adrenaline junkie. I feed off big crowds and noise.

— CURT SCHILLING, all-star pitcher

I'm in the twilight of a mediocre career.

— FRANK SULLIVAN, pitcher

Trying to sneak a fastball past Hank Aaron is like trying to sneak sunrise past a rooster.

—Curt Simmons, all-star pitcher

The mound is my personal zone. During those moments on the pitching rubber, when you have every pitch at your command working to its highest potential, you are in your own universe.

—Bill Lee, all-star pitcher nicknamed "Spaceman"

Pitching is the art of instilling fear.

—Sandy Koufax, Hall of Fame pitcher

Any delivery without control is no delivery at all.

—Charles "Ol' Hoss" Radbourn,
Hall of Fame pitcher

Johnny Sain didn't try to make you pitch like he did. He put himself in your shoes. He had allegiance to you. He made you think. He was the best pitching coach in baseball.

—JIM BOUTON, all-star pitcher and author of *Ball Four*

If it wasn't for the splitter, I'd still be a printer's assistant back in Mount Joy, Pennsylvania.

—BRUCE SUTTER, all-star pitcher

I owe my baseball success to clean living and a fast outfield.

—LEFTY GOMEZ, Hall of Fame pitcher

Every time I hold a ball in my hand and put that suit on. That's been my biggest day.

—DIZZY DEAN, Hall of Fame pitcher

Just take the ball and throw it where you want to.
Throw strikes. Home plate don't move.

—SATCHEL PAIGE, Hall of Fame pitcher

When they operated, I told them to put in a Koufax
fastball. They did—but it was Mrs. Koufax's fastball.

—TOMMY JOHN, all-star pitcher,
speaking about his arm surgery

Like drinking coffee with a fork.

—WILLIE STARGELL, Hall of Fame outfielder/first
baseman, describing hitting against Koufax

How do I pitch him? I wish I could throw the ball
under the plate.

—DON NEWCOMBE,
all-star pitcher, on pitching to Hank Aaron

I've got a lot of years to live after baseball. And I would like to live them with the complete use of my body.

—SANDY KOUFAX, Hall of Fame pitcher, announcing his retirement due to debilitating arthritis

You spend a good piece of your life gripping a baseball and in the end it turns out that it was the other way around all the time.

—JIM BOUTON, all-star pitcher

A pitcher's got to be good and he's got to be lucky to get a no hit game.

—CY YOUNG, Hall of Fame pitcher who recorded the first perfect game in 1904

When I started to throw the ball back to the pitcher harder than he was throwing to me, we changed positions.

—BERT BLYLEVEN, all-star pitcher known for a wicked curveball

I put my whole heart and soul into baseball, then one day, it was all over. When you leave baseball you leave part of your childhood behind.

—SANDY VANCE, pitcher

Good pitching will always stop good hitting, and vice versa.

—CASEY STENGEL

5th Inning

Batter Up!—
All about Hitting

Carrots may be good for my eyes, but they won't straighten out the curve ball.

—CARL FURILLO, all-star outfielder

With this batting slump I'm in, I was so happy to hit a double that I did a tap dance on second base. They tagged me between taps.

—FRENCHY BORDAGARAY, outfielder

A pitcher never gets me out. I get myself out. That's no disrespect to the pitcher, but there should be no excuse for failure. You can't have an excuse to fail.

—MIKE PIAZZA, all-star catcher

To be a good hitter you've got to do one thing—get a good ball to hit.

—ROGERS HORNSBY, Hall of Fame second baseman

There were times last year when people looked at the scoreboard and thought my batting average was the temperature.

—BUCK MARTINEZ, player and manager

I have always maintained that the best remedy for a batting slump is two wads of cotton. One for each ear.

—BILL VEECK, baseball executive

Most slumps are like the common cold. They last two weeks no matter what you do.

—TERRY KENNEDY, all-star catcher

I must admit when Reggie Jackson hit that third home run, and I was sure nobody was listening, I applauded into my glove.

—STEVE GARVEY, all-star first baseman who played for the losing Dodgers in the World Series

Baseball is the only field of endeavor where a man can succeed three times out of ten and be considered a good performer.

—TED WILLIAMS, Hall of Fame outfielder

When I stood up there as a pinch hitter, I honestly believed I was the best hitter in the game. That's the only attitude to have.

—MANNY MOTA, all-star outfielder and pinch hitter extraordinaire

I have observed that baseball is not unlike a war, and when you come right down to it, we batters are the heavy artillery.

—TY COBB, Hall of Fame outfielder

As far as I'm concerned, there is no greater pleasure in the world than walking up to the plate with men on base and knowing that you are feared.

—TED SIMMONS, all-star catcher

No one can throw a fastball past me. God could come down from Heaven, and He couldn't throw it past me.

—TED WILLIAMS, Hall of Fame outfielder

The pitcher has got only a ball. I've got a bat. So the percentage in weapons is in my favor and I let the fellow with the ball do the fretting.

—HANK AARON, Hall of Fame outfielder

Hitting is an art, but not an exact science.

—ROD CAREW, Hall of Fame infielder
who won seven American League batting titles

Hitting is 50% above the shoulders.

—TED WILLIAMS, Hall of Fame outfielder

The longer I live, the longer I realize that batting is more a mental matter than it is physical. The ability to grasp the bat, swing at the proper time, take a proper stance, all these are elemental. Batting rather is a study in psychology, a sizing up of pitcher and catcher, and observing little details that are of immense importance. It's like the study of crime, the work of a detective as he picks up clues.

—TY COBB, Hall of Fame outfielder

Your bat is your life. It's your weapon. You don't want to go into battle with anything that feels less than perfect.

—LOU BROCK, Hall of Fame outfielder known as one of the games greatest base stealers

I have already written a treatise and it reads like this; "Keep your eye clear and hit 'em where they ain't; that's all!"

—WEE WILLIE KEELER, Hall of Fame outfielder with lifetime batting average of .345

A man once told me to walk with the Lord. I'd rather walk with the bases loaded.

—KEN SINGLETON all-star outfielder, who recorded three seasons with over 100 walks

6th Inning

Playing
the Field—
Fielders Have Their Say

You start chasing a ball and your brain immediately commands your body to run forward! Bend! Scoop up the ball! Peg it to first! Then your body says, who me?

—JOE DiMAGGIO, Hall of Fame outfielder

Catching a fly ball is pleasure, but knowing what to do with it after you catch it is a business.

—TOMMY HENRICH, all-star outfielder
for the Yankees, nicknamed "Old Reliable"

Don't get me wrong, I like to hit. But there's nothing like getting out there in the outfield, running after a ball and throwing somebody out trying to take that extra base. That's real fun.

—WILLIE MAYS, Hall of Fame outfielder

Two-thirds of the earth is covered by water. The other one-third is covered by Garry Maddox.

> —RALPH KINER, Hall of Fame outfielder
> and baseball announcer

A great catch is like watching girls go by. The last one you see is always the prettiest.

> —BOB GIBSON, Hall of Fame pitcher

I never had to be lonely behind the plate, where I could talk to hitters. I also learned that by engaging them in conversation, I could sometimes distract them.

> —ROY CAMPANELLA, Hall of Fame catcher
> for the Brooklyn Dodgers

When Steve and I die, we are going to be buried in the same cemetery, 60-feet, 6-inches apart.

—TIM McCARVER, all-star catcher
referring to teammate Steve Carlton

Don Buddin should have "E6" on his license plate.

—SPORTSWRITER CLIFF KEANE
on the error-prone Red Sox shortstop

"Willie," they asked, "how do you compare this catch with other catches you've made?" "I don't compare 'em," Willie said. "I catch 'em."

—LEO DUROCHER, Hall of Fame manager,
quoting Willie Mays

The wind always seems to be blowing against catchers when they are running.

—JOE GARAGIOLA, catcher who garnered greater fame as a TV personality

No outfielder is a real workman unless he can turn his back on the ball, run his legs off and take the catch over his shoulder. Backpedaling outfielders get nowhere.

—JOE DIMAGGIO, Hall of Fame outfielder

Errors are part of my image. One night in Pittsburgh, 30,000 fans gave me a standing ovation when I caught a hot-dog wrapper on the fly.

—DICK STUART, all-star first baseman, nicknamed "Dr. Strangeglove" for his reputation as a horrible fielder

You're Out!—
Views from and about the Men in Blue

You guys are just like politicians. You're never right.

—GERALD FORD, 38th president of the United States

He didn't have a good view of the game, so I gave him a chance to watch the end of it on television.

—STAN LANDES, umpire on ejecting
Dodgers second baseman Maury Willis

Umpiring is the only profession in the world where you have to be perfect when you start and continue to improve.

—TODD GREANIER, sportswriter

Boys, I'm one of those umpires that misses 'em every once in a while. So if it's close you'd better hit it.

—CAL HUBBARD, Hall of Fame umpire, and the only man elected to the baseball, college football, and professional football Halls of Fame

One thing there is that affords a baseball umpire consolation, and that is the thought that he can die only once, and then never more.

—*THE SPORTING NEWS*, 1888

There are no close plays. A man is always out or safe, or it is a ball or a strike, and the umpire, if he is a good man and knows his business, is always right. For instance, I am always right.

—SILK O'LOUGHLIN, umpire who called a league-leading seven no-hitters

I never saw an umpire change a decision he made 40 seconds ago, much less 40 years ago.

—GOOSE GOSLIN, Hall of Fame outfielder

I'm a Christian. But I have no problem with umpires. I love 'em all. I'm at peace with the world. Except on close plays.

—EARL WEAVER, Hall of Fame manager

I have never questioned the integrity of an umpire. Their eyesight, yes.

—LEO DUROCHER, Hall of Fame manager

You're out, and you're ugly, too.

—DURWOOD MERRILL, umpire

Ideally, the umpire should combine the integrity of a Supreme Court justice, the physical agility of an acrobat, the endurance of Job, and the imperturbability of Buddha

—*TIME MAGAZINE*, 1961

Son, when you pitch a strike Mr. Hornsby will let you know.

—BILL KLEM, Hall of Fame umpire
to a rookie pitcher

My favorite umpire is a dead one.

—JOHNNY EVERS, Hall of Fame second baseman

Never change a decision, never stop to talk to a man. Make 'em play ball and keep their mouths shut…people will be on your side and you'll be called the King of Umpires.

—Bob Ferguson, player, manager, and umpire

Ed, you're the second best umpire in the league. The other 23 are tied for first.

—Carl Yastrzemski, Hall of Fame outfielder
to umpire Ed Runge

Many baseball fans look at an umpire as a sort of necessary evil to the luxury of baseball, like the odor that follows an automobile.

—Christy Mathewson, Hall of Fame pitcher

Baseball is the only sport that lets the managers and the coaches go out onto the field and rant and rave.

—DURWOOD MERRILL, umpire

An angry player can't argue with the back of an umpire who is walking away.

—BILL KLEM, Hall of Fame umpire

8th Inning

A View
from the Bench—
Coaches, Managers, and
Owners Speak Out

I'm happy for him. That is, if you think becoming a big league manager is a good thing to have happen to you.

—WALT ASTON, manager, on hearing the news that Gil Hodges was also becoming a big-league manager

The fan is the one who suffers. He cheers a guy to a .350 season, then watches that player sign with another team. When you destroy fan loyalties, you destroy everything.

—FRANK ROBINSON, Hall of Fame outfielder, talking about free agency

Being a coach is like being the Queen of England. It's just a title. Coaches mostly hit fungoes.

—BOB GIBSON, Hall of Fame pitcher, on being hired as an assistant pitching coach

Girls used to come up to me and say, "My sister loves you." Now they say, "My mother loves you."

—LEE MAZZILLI, player and coach
known for his good looks

I told them you're playing for the name on the front of your uniform, not the one on the back. Of course, you have to believe you're the best player in the world as well, just don't tell anyone about it.

—TOMMY LASORDA, Hall of Fame manager's
advice to his Japanese baseball team,
the 2001 Osaka Kintetsu Buffaloes

If you're not prepared, it's not pressure you feel, it's fear.

—BRUCE BOCHY, player and manager

I've come to the conclusion that the two most important things in life are good friends and a good bullpen.

—BOB LEMON, Hall of Fame pitcher and manager

There are certain things that can't be bought: a mother's love, loyalty, friendship, and a left-handed pitcher who can throw strikes.

—CASEY STENGEL, Hall of Fame manager

Statistics are like bikinis—they show a lot, but never everything.

—LOU PINIELLA, player and manager

Bad baseball players make good managers.

—EARL WEAVER, Hall of Fame manager

There are three things the average man thinks he can do better than anyone else: build a fire, run a hotel and manage a baseball team.

—ROCKY BRIDGES,
all-star player and minor league manager

I've worked for Charlie (Finley) and I've worked for George Steinbrenner and I've survived to tell about it. Not many others can make that statement.

—EDDIE LOPAT, all-star pitcher, coach,
manager, general manager, and scout

Just a fad. It'll never last after the novelty wears off.

—ED BARROW, Hall of Fame manager,
on night baseball

Good luck is what is left over after intelligence and effort have combined at their best.

—BRANCH RICKEY, baseball executive

Remember, half the lies they tell about the Dodgers aren't true.

—WALTER O'MALLEY, famed owner of the Brooklyn and Los Angeles Dodgers

Earl Weaver called Ken Singleton into his office
    and asked him:
"Is something wrong?"
"No, nothing's wrong,"
"Are you sick?"
"No"
"Are you tired?"
"No."
"Well, I'm sick and tired of you not hitting!"

—EARL WEAVER, Hall of Fame manager to Ken Singleton, all-star player

"I apologize to all the village idiots of America. He's the nation's idiot."

> —CHARLES FINLEY, owner, on calling
> Commissioner Bowie Kuhn the village idiot

I was a victim of circumcision.

> —PETE VUKOVICH, pitching coach,
> on being thrown out of a game

One reporter asked me about the chemistry on this club. I told him I didn't even pass biology in high school.

> —JIM FREY, manager

He had the ability of taking a bad situation and making it immediately worse.

> —BRANCH RICKEY, baseball executive,
> on manager Leo Durocher

If I ever find a pitcher who has heat, a good curve, and a slider, I might seriously consider marrying him, or at least proposing.

—Sparky Anderson, Hall of Fame manager
who retired with 2,194 wins

From the Pen to the Plate—
Writers' Tribute to Baseball

I don't care whether or not it is childish. Long before I possessed any capacity to examine myself or the reason for the game's appeal to me, I loved it.

—JAMES T. FARRELL, novelist

Baseball is the writer's game, and its train of thought, we come to sense, is a shuttle, carrying us constantly forward to the next pitch or inning, or the sudden double into the left-field corner, but we keep hold of the other half of our ticket, for the return trip on the same line.

—ROGER ANGELL, author

There is something uniquely American about hitting one out of the park.

—DICK YOUNG, sportswriter

Say this much for big-league baseball—it is beyond question the greatest conversation piece ever invented in America.

—BRUCE CATTON, historian

I find baseball fascinating. It strikes me as a native American ballet, a totally different dance form. Nearly every move in baseball—the windup, the pitch, the motion of the infielder—is different from other games. Next to the triple play, baseball's double play is the most exciting and graceful thing in sports.

—ALISTAIR COOKE, journalist

It is an old baseball joke that big-inning baseball is affirmed in the Bible, in Genesis. In the big inning, God created....

—GEORGE WILL, writer

He was frank to the point of being cruel, and subtle as a belch.

—LEE ALLEN, writer, on Rogers Hornsby

Baseball is the very symbol, the outward and visible expression of the drive and push and rush and struggle of the raging, tearing, booming nineteenth century.

—MARK TWAIN, writer and humorist

Well, it's our game; that's the chief fact in connection with it; America's game; it has the snap, go, and fling of the American atmosphere; it belongs as much to our institutions, fits into them as significantly as our Constitution's laws; is just as important in the sum total of our historic life.

—WALT WHITMAN, poet

Fanaticism? No. Writing is exciting and baseball is like writing. You can never tell with either how it will go or what you will do.

—MARIANNE MOORE, poet

Baseball is the most intellectual game because most of the action goes on in your head.

—HENRY KISSINGER, diplomat and author

The game of baseball has always been linked in my mind with the mystic texture of childhood, with the sounds and smells of summer nights and with the memories of my father.

—DORIS KEARNS GOODWIN, historian

Here is a game in which there is no clock, the defense holds the ball, though it has rigid rules, every park is different, the greatest heroes fail seven times out of ten, a game that's born in the spring dies in the fall. This is life.

—KEN BURNS, documentary filmmaker

They can't yank a novelist like they can a pitcher. A novelist has to go the full nine, even if it kills him.

—ERNEST HEMINGWAY, writer

Who is this Baby Ruth? And what does she do?

—GEORGE BERNARD SHAW, writer

All literary men are Red Sox fans. To be a Yankee fan in literary society is to endanger your life.

—JOHN CHEEVER, writer

All winter long I am one for whom the bell is
   tolling;
I can arouse no interest in basketball, indoor fly
   casting or bowling;
The sports pages are strictly no soap,
And until the cry of Play Ball! I simply mope

—OGDEN NASH, humorist and writer

A beautiful game, superbly played… Yes, a grand
game, a game entirely worthy of its reputation.

—A BRITISH WRITER'S reaction to
seeing his first baseball game in 1912

Ninety feet between bases is perhaps as close as
man has ever gotten to perfection.

—RED SMITH, sports writer

Fenway Park in Boston is a lyric little bandbox of a ballpark. Everything is painted green and seems in curiously sharp focus, like the inside of an old-fashioned peeping-type Easter egg.

—JOHN UPDIKE, writer

Whoever wants to know the heart and mind of America had better learn baseball, the rules and realities of the game—and do it by watching first some high school or small-town teams.

—JACQUES BARZUN, writer, historian, and educator

It is designed to break your heart. The game begins in spring, when everything else begins again, and blossoms in the summer, filling the afternoons and evenings, and then as soon as the chill rains come, it stops and leaves you to face the fall alone.

—A. BARTLETT GIAMATTI, educator, writer, and former commissioner of baseball

I have snatched my share of joys from the grudging hands of Fate as I have jogged along, but never has life held for me anything quite so entrancing as baseball.

—CLARENCE DARROW, lawyer

[Baseball stimulates] a childish and orgiastic local pride, a typical American weakness....

—H. L. MENCKEN, writer

Baseball is dull only to dull minds.

—RED BARBER, baseball announcer

Baseball is religion without the mischief.

—THOMAS BOSWELL, sports writer

Nothing flatters me more than to have it assumed that I could write prose unless it be to have it assumed that I once pitched a baseball with distinction.

—ROBERT FROST, poet

He was built along the lines of a beer keg and not unfamiliar with its contents.

—SHIRLEY POVICH, writer on Hack Wilson

Wrigley field is a Peter Pan of a ballpark... It's never grown up (or) old.

—E. M. SWIFT, sportswriter

Oh, somewhere in this favored land the sun is
    shining bright;
The band is playing somewhere, and somewhere
    hearts are light;
And somewhere men are laughing, and little
    children shout;
But there is no joy in Mudville—mighty Casey
    has struck out.

   —ERNEST LAWRENCE THAYER, "Casey at the Bat"

From the Oval Office to the Diamond:

Presidents on Baseball

I don't know a lot about politics, but I know a lot about baseball.

—RICHARD M. NIXON,
37th president of the United States

I do all I can for them. I even pray for them each night. I hope the Supreme Court doesn't declare that unconstitutional.

—LYNDON B. JOHNSON, 36th president of the United States on the Washington Senators

A couple of years ago they told me I was too young to be president and you were too old to be playing baseball. But we fooled them, and we're still fooling them.

—JOHN F. KENNEDY, 35th president of the United States, to St. Louis Cardinals' first baseman Stan Musial, at the 1962 All-Star Game

I honestly feel that it would be best for the country to keep baseball going. There will be fewer people unemployed and everybody will work longer hours and harder than ever before, and that means they ought to have a chance for recreation and for taking their minds off their work even more than before.

—FRANKLIN ROOSEVELT, 32nd president of the
United States in a letter to baseball commissioner
clearing the way for the game to continue
during World War II

Next to religion, baseball has furnished a greater impact on American life than any other institution.

—HERBERT HOOVER,
31st president of the United States

"Hello, Joe? It's Frank. Giants three, Dodgers nothing."

> —FRANKLIN D. ROOSEVELT, 32nd president of the United States, in a telephone call to Joseph Stalin

This is really more fun than being president. I really do love baseball and I wish we could do this out on the lawn every day.

> —RONALD REAGAN, 40th president of the United States on playing ball with old-timers during National Baseball Month

If I had it to do over again, I'd name Casey secretary of state. The essence of diplomacy is to confuse the opposition. The opposition never knew what Casey was talking about. Stengel always knew.

> —RICHARD NIXON, 37th president of the United States

I couldn't see well enough to play when I was a boy, so they gave me a special job—they made me the umpire.

—HARRY S TRUMAN,
33rd president of the United States

With grace and steely determination, he pushed open a door that should never have been closed and held it open for the countless talented young men and women who followed him.

—BILL CLINTON, 42nd president of the United States
on the achievement of Jackie Robinson

I'd watch a lot of baseball on radio.

—GERALD R. FORD,
38th president of the United States

When I was a small boy in Kansas, a friend of mine and I went fishing and as we sat there in the warmth of the summer afternoon on a river bank, we talked about what we wanted to do when we grew up. I told him that I wanted to be a real major league baseball player, a genuine professional like Honus Wagner. My friend said that he'd like to be president of the United States. Neither of us got our wish.

—Dwight D. Eisenhower,
34th president of the United States

The game of baseball is a clean, straight game, and it summons to its presence everybody who enjoys clean, straight athletics. It furnishes amusement to the thousands and thousands.

—William Taft, 27th president of the United States

I never dreamed about being president, I wanted to be Willie Mays.

—GEORGE W. BUSH,
43rd president of the United States

When money comes in at the gate, sport flies out at the window.

—THEODORE ROOSEVELT,
26th president of the United States

Our National Game.

—ANDREW JOHNSON,
17th president of the United States

I am glad to hear of them coming, but they will have to wait a few minutes till I get my turn at bat.

—ABRAHAM LINCOLN,
16th president of the United States

Yogi's been an inspiration to me. Not only because of his baseball skills, of course, but because of the enduring mark he left on the English language. Some of the press corps here even think he is my speech writer.

—George W. Bush,
43rd president of the United States

Who's on First—
Hollywood on Baseball

There's no crying in baseball.

—TOM HANKS, actor in *A League of Their Own*

A friend gave me seats to the World Series. From where I sat, the game was just a rumor.

—HENNY YOUNGMAN, comedian

Bat day seems like a good idea, but I question the advisability of giving bats in the Bronx to 40,000 Yankee fans.

—AARON BACALL, comedian

Fred Patek is so small that when he was born his father passed out cigar butts.

—JOEY ADAMS, comedian,
on the one-time Royals' shortstop

When we played softball, I'd steal second base, feel guilty, and go back.

    —WOODY ALLEN, writer, director, and actor

If the Cincinnati Reds were really the first major league baseball team, who did they play?

    —GEORGE CARLIN, comedian

If the World Series goes seven games, it will be NBC's longest running show this fall.

    —JOHNNY CARSON, talk-show host

If Pete Rose bets on prison softball games, will he be barred from jail for life?

    —JAY LENO, talk-show host

A hot dog at the ballpark is better than steak at the Ritz.

—HUMPHREY BOGART, actor,
in a film ad for organized baseball

There have been only two authentic geniuses in the world, Willie Mays and Willie Shakespeare.

—TALLULAH BANKHEAD, actor

My last miracle was the '69 Mets.

—GEORGE BURNS, actor in *Oh, God!*

That ball got out of here in a hurry. Anything going that fast better have a damn stewardess on it, don't you think?

—KEVIN COSTNER, actor in *Bull Durham*

I never thought about being a writer as I grew up; a writer wasn't something to be. An outfielder was something to be. Most of what I know about style I learned from Roberto Clemente.

—JOHN SAYLES, writer and director

It gives me a chance to "smile out loud" under God's clear sky and to take in life-giving breaths of fresh air every time one empties the lungs with a lusty cheer.

—LILLIAN RUSSELL, actor

The one constant through all the years has been baseball. America has rolled by like an army of steamrollers. It's been erased like a blackboard, rebuilt, and erased again. But baseball has marked the time. This field, this game, is part of our past. It reminds us of all that once was good, and what could be again.

—JAMES EARL JONES, actor in *Field of Dreams*